YOU CHANGE, THEY CHANGE

HOW TO TAKE CONTROL OF YOUR LIFE BY LOSING CONTROL OVER OTHERS.

Kim McDonnel

You Change, They Change
How to take control of your life
by Kim McDonnel
Copyright © 2018 Kim McDonnel
Published by SkillBites LLC
All rights reserved.

This publication contains the opinions and ideas of its author. It is intended to provide helpful and informative material on the subjects addressed in the publication. Even though the steps outlined in this book will allow you to move forward with the goals in your life, there is no guarantee that these will be achieved by reading the book. The author of this book does not dispense medical advice or prescribe the use of any technique as a form of treatment for physical, emotional, or medical problems without the advice of a physician, either directly or indirectly. The intent of the author is to offer information of a general nature to help you in your quest for emotional and spiritual well-being. In the event you use any of the information in this book for yourself, the author and publisher assume no responsibility for your actions.

No part of this book may be reproduced or transmitted in any form or by any means whatsoever without written permission from the author, except in the case of brief quotations embodied in critical articles and reviews.

ISBN-10: 1-942489-55-2
ISBN-13: 978-1-942489-55-9

TESTIMONIALS

Kim has learned through her own journey to healing and transformation that love conquers all. She is now sharing the tools she used to get her to this state of awesomeness. Living a life of non-judgement and in balance is very Oola! What a blessing this work will be to those who choose to be the change.

Dave Braun, author of *Oola: Find Balance in an Unbalanced World* and *Oola for Women: Find Balance in an Unbalanced World*, Salt Lake City, Utah

Kim McDonnel takes a new direction in helping us to drive real change in our lives. I especially loved her focus on ownership and how we can't grow if we don't own who we are today and who we want to be tomorrow. The open-ended questions Kim asks in this book challenged me to look deeper inside for answers that had been there all along, but I just didn't have the guidance to get there. This book pushed me, and that is a really good thing!

Eric Walton, author of *Downline Leadership: Blueprint for Network Marketing Leaders*, Phoenix, Arizona

I love this wonderful book! It is a powerful spiritual self- help book that will inspire you to face your personal truths to evoke positive change. Kim's giving spirit and ability to provide simple step by step exercises to guide you to open your heart and mind to endless possibilities is truly a gift from God.

Sue Gorman,
Covington, Louisiana

As I approach the one year anniversary of my first scan and appointment with you, I have a much more clear view of who I am. You have taught me so many things that have helped me grow with my partner, my business and with my family. I cannot count the times you've said to me, "You Change, They Change" as I told you a story about an encounter at home, work or with siblings. My partner of nearly twenty years, who I swore would NEVER embrace many of these principals, is seeking to learn how to make some of the same changes I've made. Your guidance on this path has been instrumental in strengthening our relationship. Thank you for sharing your time, advice, guidance, love and wisdom with others.

Trey Buerger,
New Orleans, Louisiana

The past 8 months have been some of the darkest and also most beautiful days I've ever experienced in my life. Since the beginning of these 8 months, Kim has extended such love, kindness, encouragement, wisdom and knowledge towards me. Her friendship has been such a gift! I am incredibly grateful for her voice and the knowledge she has shared with me, both from her own experience and from wisdom she has gained from others. I know she has poured her heart and soul into this book and I am grateful that many more people will be able to learn and grow from her words that are sure to be saturated with love as her heart is passionately geared towards extending health and healing to everyone she encounters.

Faith B Wilson,
Covington, Louisiana

It is not only Kim's wise words which inspire, but her actions! I am proud and blessed to call this beautiful, strong woman my friend for over 20 years. Watching her grow as a wife, mother, and spiritual counselor have truly motivated me to grow. Kim perseveres through everything life throws at her all while helping everyone else around her do the same. She has taught me that life is a journey we must embrace; there's no time to harbor regret!

Jenny Gomez,
Abita Springs, Louisiana

During my time with Kim, she would minister to me with love, grace, and wisdom. She has channeled her past hurts, pains and lessons learned into teachable moments and fresh perspective for people she encounters. Kim is able to look beyond the surface level with her deep intuition and help guide a person to find inner healing. Kim's love for God and love for people shines through her work and I am so very grateful to have a friend in her.

Hailey Aliff,
Young Living Royal Crown Diamond,
Covington, Louisiana

I can't say enough how much Kim has helped me through one of the darkest times of my life. Being my cheerleader, supporter, and calling me out when she needed to. Encouraging me not to blame others but to look at myself first, forgive, and accept to be the change I wanted to see. Her words and tools have been life changing.

Leslie Nobles,
Baton Rouge, LA

I met Kim several years ago and have watched her grow and become an inspiration to others. She is incredibly knowledgeable and enjoys sharing her insight and knowledge to help others. She has helped me grow as an individual as well as inspired me to lean in to life. Her motto "You Change, They Change" is absolutely true. I have seen this first hand and it is a blessing. I feel privileged to know her and to be the recipient of her wisdom. Kim, you are an amazingly strong woman. Thank you for caring & sharing!

Beckie Stein,
Covington, LA

Kim McDonnel has been such a blessing in my life. I've had the privilege of working with her in business, and as a health coach, and her wisdom has been so impactful upon my life! So many times when we encounter difficulties in relationships, we want others to change first in order for unity to be restored. I love the idea of us first looking inward, and taking personal responsibility for our own growth, instead of waiting on others to change. Thank you, Kim, for sharing your God given wisdom so unselfishly, and so freely with others!

Stephanie Post Long,
Covington, LA

You Change, They Change

I am blessed to have met Kim. She has become a friend, mentor and someone I truly cherish. She makes time to speak to me and always seems to know the right thing to say whether it's regarding my wellness, emotional or family issues. I am still learning and will continue to learn from her, others, and myself. If I change they around me will change.

Nicole Schlaudecker,
New Orleans, LA

TABLE OF CONTENTS

CHAPTER 1 .... **1**
Own Your Truth in Order to Be Trusted

<u>Daily Affirmation</u>

I am living my purpose and passion

CHAPTER 2 .... **9**
Check Your Intentions

<u>Daily Affirmation</u>

I am setting good intentions daily

CHAPTER 3 .... **15**
Judge Not, Lest You Be Judged

<u>Daily Affirmation</u>

I am accepting of others, knowing we are all perfectly made but have acquired wounds to heal

CHAPTER 4 .... **21**
It's Not About YOU!

<u>Daily Affirmation</u>

I am seeing everyone's situation as their own personal journey in finding their truth

CHAPTER 5 .... **29**
    Look in The Mirror

> ### Daily Affirmation
>
> *I am understanding of myself and others, with love and acceptance*

CHAPTER 6 .... **37**
    Speaking a New Language

> ### Daily Affirmation
>
> *I know who I am and what I want and am keeping my focus on what's good and positive*

CHAPTER 7 .... **45**
    Rewrite Your Story

> ### Daily Affirmation
>
> *I am seeing my past as the perfect canvas to paint the picture of who I am now, full of compassion, joy, and love*

CHAPTER 8 .... **51**
    Defining Success

> ### Daily Affirmation
>
> *I am successfully living a balanced life full of love and acceptance*

PREFACE

Why Change?

Let me guess—you decided to read this book because you want to change something or someone in your life. I understand that feeling, having walked that path myself, and I honor your desire to live a more fulfilled life. We all want to be happy and successful in every area of our lives, but we don't live in isolation, and our happiness and success are often interconnected with those dearest to us. The question then becomes: how can we be happy if those we love are not?

Let's be honest. At different times in our lives, each of us has determined that we've somehow gotten "stuck" in our lives, and we want to get "unstuck" from situations or patterns of behavior that are no longer making us happy or successful. As a result, we commit to personal change in order to find that place of happiness and success once again. However, it's not just about us, is it? Our lives are entwined with others, and they're often the ones whom we allow to affect our patterns of behavior. It's easy for us to put the blame on others, identifying the changes *they* need to make, but is that really fair?

When we can only see what others are or *are not* doing or saying, have we fallen into the trap of focusing on changing them to meet our expectations when we should really be focusing on changing ourselves? We all crave community, love, and respect, but do we give these things, especially to the same degree that we desire or even demand them for ourselves? Are we living up to our expectations of other people? Take some time to ponder these questions as you read further, and ask yourself how you can be the change you wish to see in others.

To live a life of passion and purpose we have to know what that looks like for us personally. The bottom line is that we're solely accountable and responsible for our own behaviors, actions, and responses, and nobody else's.

In some ways, this is life's greatest lesson: how to honor ourselves while still honoring others. Some of our most challenging relationships are with the people we love the most—our spouses, children, and parents. We tend to see all the negatives that need to be fixed in them, which leads to an even greater negative perception of their behaviors. It's very hard to love and accept a person as they are when you see so much more that they could be. This frustration and sadness can make you feel hopeless. Unfortunately, this negative energy only repels the person further from where you want them to be.

The purpose of this book is to help us learn how we can stop this negative pattern. Words, meditations, and journaling exercises have all been included to help you put these teachings into practice, allowing you to let go and shift your energy from negative to positive. You'll also learn positive actions you can take that may in turn create personal change.

To help you get the most support for the changes that will naturally occur, please refer to this book's corresponding course located on my website at www.kimmcdonnel.com before and during each chapter. You will be prompted throughout the book with the keywords "Journal" or "Reflect" and the statement "Let's Make this Personal." On my website, you will find guided meditations and journaling exercises. If you need additional support, I will be offering both one-on-one and group sessions, which can be scheduled from my website under the "Coaching" tab.

For me, personal faith in God has been a critical component driving change in my life, so you'll notice as you read that I refer to God. You should think of whatever higher power you believe in on these occasions. I think that we all need to believe in something bigger than ourselves to give us strength and hope and to guide us on this journey in life. Whatever that means for you is accepted by me, as I hope we can all accept each other's beliefs.

As you begin to make changes in yourself, you'll probably experience the following scenarios:

- Some people who love and respect you will honor the changes they see in you and will follow your example to begin to make changes in themselves.
- The people who haven't faced the need for similar changes in themselves may become uncomfortable around you.
- Some people will be indifferent to the changes in you.

We'll deal with each of these. When you change, they change, so let's make it for the better. Welcome to your healing journey toward creating positive change!

CHAPTER 1

Own Your Truth in Order to Be Trusted

Daily Affirmation

I am living my purpose and passion

When I speak about owning your truth, I'm referring to your instincts, beliefs, and God-given intuitions. When you are consistent with your thoughts and actions, other people see you as trustworthy. Learning how to own your truth comes from your own sense of self-worth.

When you have feelings, put those feelings into words. Say what you mean at the time you feel it so that it can be dealt with then, not stuck in your head as a rumination that goes around and around like a broken record. So many times, we assume others know what we're thinking or feeling as if we've told them those things out loud. We shouldn't expect people to be able to read our minds or assume that they know how we're feeling in that moment.

Personally, I'm a very sensitive and empathetic person who easily picks up on and responds to what others are sensing and feeling. That led me to have a very confused childhood, and has created even more difficulty for me as an adult. My assumption that others would as easily be aware of and responsive to my needs—without my having to ask for what I needed out loud—caused me to continually feel disappointed and unloved.

Feeling unloved or disappointed in how I was treated prevented me from asking for what I needed or wanted out of a fear of not being accepted. This fear also caused me to not be able to say when I felt hurt. However, this unwillingness to express myself openly was a form of dishonesty and manipulation. Because I wasn't owning what I wanted, I was trying to make others love and accept me by doing what I thought they wanted. Healthy relationships can't thrive when they're founded on hidden dishonesty.

Honesty breeds trust. Are you seen by others as honest and trustworthy? Do you trust others? Do you trust yourself? You won't trust others if you can't trust yourself to be honest, and you can't be honest with yourself if you don't know who you are and what you want. If you've only been doing what others ask or expect of you, it can be difficult, if not impossible, to identify and get in touch with your honest wants and needs.

Take some time to journal what you want your day to look like, then your week and your year. Do you find this hard to do? If so, it may help to spend some time feeding into your likes so you can find your passion. Take the time to do the daily meditation linked with this chapter to open your mind to the possibilities God has in store for you.

If you feel that you're not trusted by others, it may be because you haven't been following through on your promises. Even small promises that aren't kept can cause people to perceive you as untrustworthy. Not following through when you're a people-pleaser is typically due to exhaustion from trying to be what you think others need while ignoring or not knowing what you need.

Here are some examples you may not have associated with trust, but which can undermine others' perceptions of your trustworthiness:

- Not calling someone back after you said you would.
- Doing the things you say you don't do, such as texting while driving, gossiping, or passing blame.
- Committing to be there for a friend or organization, then failing to follow through with your commitment.
- Being perpetually late.

It's hard to live up to all the pressure to be what you think everyone wants and needs in all situations, especially because it often results in your extending yourself beyond your capabilities. Something will eventually have to give, and when it does, you'll be seen as untrustworthy.

Let's Make This Personal:

- What are you passionate about? To answer this, ask yourself this: if you could spend time doing something that is fulfilling and that makes you happy, what would it be?
- What is preventing you from living your passion?

- Where are you overextended? (Overfilling your time with busywork, commitments to others, crutches or vices.)
- Where are you over-promising and under-delivering? Ask yourself why.
- Where are you doing acts of service in order to be accepted and valued by others (believing you're supposed to be everything to everyone)?
- Journal why you may be trying to portray perfection in order to be thought of highly by others.
- Who in your life do you perceive as being perfect?
- What makes you believe them to be perfect?

Unfortunately, when we overextend ourselves, we become forgetful, overwhelmed, and anxiety-ridden. That causes us to then fail to follow through on our commitments to others as well as ourselves. This results in our being seen as someone who can't be relied on.

Being untrustworthy was the last thing I wanted others to think of me. I didn't lie, cheat, or steal. I had high standards and morals. Why would anyone *not* trust me? It never occurred to me that, because I wasn't really the person they had thought I was and because I really didn't know who I was myself, I actually *was* someone who couldn't be trusted.

Growing up as a people-pleaser, I said what I thought people wanted me to say in order for them to approve of me. I also tried to be what I thought people wanted me to be so that I would feel accepted and affirmed by others. I thought keeping the peace meant giving up mine.

Journal about a few times that this concept of owning your truth has been an issue in your life. Ask yourself where or in whom you've seen this type of behavior. What has been the catalyst or motivating factor that prevented you from owning your truth in those instances? Could the fear of rejection, feelings of unworthiness, or sense of vulnerability have been the cause?

We each need to take the time to learn how to say no. It's a crucial part of being the man or woman of your word whom you want to be. Saying no enables you to stop overextending so you can give of yourself in the ways you want to be given to—

with honesty and without strings, attachments to outcomes, or anxiety.

An area where it's especially important to own your truth so you will be trusted is in raising your children. They need to be able to take you at your word, knowing you'll do what you've promised. Not only that, they also need this modeled so that they learn how to apply this concept in their own lives.

Telling our children to do things we're not doing ourselves is lying to them. Here are some examples of inconsistencies I've noticed in our society today when it comes to raising our children. Are you guilty of saying these but doing differently?

Don't text and drive.

Don't spend so much time on your phone.

Don't drink and drive.

Don't speed.

Don't raise your voice at me.

Don't disrespect your father/mother/teacher.

Don't talk about other people.

Don't talk about yourself that way.

I could list a hundred more, but I think you get what I'm saying. We have to lead by example in order for our kids to trust us.

This concept has been an enormous game changer for me as a mother. Our society has arrived at a place where what used to be unacceptable is now the norm. This makes it difficult to set healthy boundaries and not feel different or judgmental. But if I'm feeling this way, so are many others. It simply takes someone owning their truth to set the tone for others to follow.

Children sense and see more than you think. When you tell them one thing but do otherwise, you become a hypocrite. We're all going to make mistakes; however, it's repeated inconsistent behavior that will give your children cause not to trust you.

When you do mess up, make sure you turn that mistake into something good. Be vulnerable, apologize, and teach them that no one is perfect; everyone makes mistakes. It's how we courageously rise up and accept responsibility that makes the mistake something worth having happened.

While we're on this subject of being trusted as parents, we can't miss addressing little white lies. They're unacceptable in raising children. Psalm 15:4 in part reads, "Swear to your own hurt." The idea is that, if you make a promise, keep it even if it isn't convenient. We can take that further and say that if you've made a mistake, own up to it in truth instead of covering it up with a "white lie." It can be painful and sometimes embarrassing to choose to be honest, but your children will learn from your example of integrity.

It's important to live your life before your children as a model of integrity. For example, return the item that the clerk mistakenly didn't charge you for when you checked out. Tell someone when they drop money out of their purse. Tell the truth, even when it hurts to do so. Be the example you want your children and future generations to follow. You'll experience the positive impact of reduced stress, anxiety, and worry, which will leave you more energy to do the things you want to do each day.

Take some time to reflect on anything that came up for you while you were reading this chapter.

- In what areas of your life are you living a lie?
- How are you putting on a facade of perfection that your children believe they must maintain and measure up to?
- Where are you expecting them to do what you haven't done yourself?
- Listen to the voice telling you to own your truth, not society's. What is it speaking to you personally?
- What are you passionate about and how can you find your happiness in it?

If you're having a hard time with owning your truth, it may be time to check your intentions.

CHAPTER 2

Check Your Intentions

Daily Affirmation

I am setting good intentions daily

There are so many times when we get caught up in what society expects or what we think we should be that we come across as disingenuous or inauthentic. Checking our intentions before we act, speak, or text will set our focus on the outcome and clear up any negative energy that could derail what we really want to achieve.

When we act first and think second, we lose sight of our wants and needs. Living an unintentional life gets us nowhere fast, and we'll feel disconnected and rejected from ourselves and others as a result. There's nothing wrong with being a go-getter and living our passions. It is when we're not living our truths, instead trying to morph into someone else's, that it can get messy.

Taking the time to decipher how we want to show up in the world and practicing that behavior will solidify who we are and how we're seen by others. We don't want to get so caught up in trying to be what others expect us to be that we lose who we are and who we truly want to be. Let me explain further with a pretty common example.

You text your husband who's at work, saying, "Are you about to leave?" He says, "No, I have about an hour left before I can get away." You say, "OK," but you get off the phone aggravated. You're hungry and want to eat dinner, and he's not going to be home to eat anytime soon, so now you are angry with him. Sound familiar?

What were your true intentions when you texted? You were hungry and wanted to know how soon he would be available to eat with you. Did you relay that intention to him in your text? No! Do you think you should be angry with him or yourself? I'll give you the answer—YOURSELF! You weren't clear on your intentions and you set him up for failure.

Here's an example of an intentional text: "Hi honey, I'm getting hungry. How long will you be? Should I wait for you to eat with me?" This text communicates your intentions with clarity, is absent of passive-aggressive behavior, owns your truth, and asks for what you need. In it, you owned your intentions. Good job!

Unintentional behavior can lead to passive-aggressive actions. When you're aggravated with an outcome, you may say things to shine light on your anger, but if you don't feel you can discuss why, you leave your reasons for your anger unspoken, waiting for the other person to figure it out and apologize. This is being passive-aggressive.

Direct people speak in plain English. Children only hear you and listen when you are direct. Being subtle and indirect with your intentions can negatively impact your relationship with your spouse, as well as your ability to parent your child and ultimately have a peaceful household.

Let me share another example. Let's say that you meet a friend of a friend. You know this friend is influential and "in the know." She can help you grow your business; however, you know she's better friends with your competitor. You intentionally friend her and not-so-subtly get digs in on your competitor, but she sees through your actions to your true intentions. The end result? You look bad, desperate, and dishonorable.

What were your intentions? Had you really liked this person for who she was and not what she could do for you, maybe you would have gotten a friendship with a side of business. When you check your intentions and deem them as good, you infuse them with healthy, positive energy. People want that, crave that, and will see that in you. When you let jealousy, hatred, distrust, and manipulation lead your intentions, you infuse that negative energy into your aura and people will be repelled by you.

Let's Make This Personal:

- Take a moment to write down some scenarios where you weren't acting with intention.
- Reflect on how you could have changed that scenario to be one of intention.
- Where have you seen that in your past?

Living intentionally may take work if you were raised by a parent figure who didn't practice intentional parenting. This can come in the form of whining for what you want, guilting others to get what you want, and/or shaming others into submission. Have you heard the language I'm speaking about? Let me share a couple of examples:

- Are you sure you want to wear that? You may get cold and I think you'd be more comfortable in that sweater and pants instead of that short, tight dress.
- Aren't they going to tell you something about that hair in your eyes?

Where have you heard this or similar conversations before?

My mentor Tonya Nichols had a theory that this language originated sometime in the early 1940s, when women went to work while men went to war. Women became independent and multitasked, raising a family and bringing home a paycheck. When the men came home, there was an imbalance in the roles. Women wanted validation for the jobs they had been doing without the help of their husbands, and men wanted to reclaim their roles as "man of the house." Women also were not afforded equal pay for equal work.

As a result, women learned to use subtle and not so subtle innuendos to get their messages across and to get what they wanted. This, in turn, caused an inauthenticity to develop in generations to follow as women continued to experience a constant struggle to have a voice and to ask for help, love, sex, respect, and more. You name it, women didn't own it. They beat around the bush, coerced, and manipulated to get the outcomes they wanted because they certainly couldn't use their words to speak their truth—no one would listen or place value on their thoughts, opinions, and desires.

Let me paint a pretty common scenario I've come across, to illustrate my point. Let's say a housewife of that decade wanted to buy herself new shoes, however her husband, who comments on her spending habits, is the only one bringing in a paycheck. She buys the shoes and hides them so as not to have a confrontation over her spending. She wants to wear her new shoes but is in fear of her husband asking where she got them, so she either keeps them hidden or she wears them and lies about how she got them. She would get her shoes, but would also be left with her dirty little secret to stress her out and ruminate on. Would that be healthy for her? Do you think that the stress of her lie would show up in her body? YES, and it did!

Soon after that generation came a generation who relied on antidepressants to cope with motherhood. Men were working longer hours, leaving their wives home to deal with everything else, including trying to be what society deemed "perfect." Perfect wives made for unhappy, neglected children who never learned how to own their truth and live with intention.

We need to ask ourselves, in what ways are we repeating the mistakes of that generation? Are we trying to manipulate situations or people to get what we want because we're afraid to say what that is? Are we so exhausted in mind and body that we need an escape yet don't feel worthy of one? Ask yourself if this is true of you, and if so, why? Have you not owned your voice? What are your true intentions? Own them, speak them, honor yourself, and teach your children to do the same.

Let's Make This Personal:

- Take a few minutes and write down what you really want, from dinner to sex and everything in between. Your spouse and children can't read your mind. They want you to tell them what's important to you! In fact, they *need* you to tell them because they don't know what you're thinking! More importantly, you need to know what you want and be brave enough to ask for it directly with intention.
- Practice saying what you want and need, and see what shows up! You may find that you don't have an excuse to be mad or pouty anymore. If that's the case, then you're left with a question of why you're still unhappy. That's when the real deep healing work begins! Let's begin with who or what you are judging for the answers.

CHAPTER 3

Judge Not, Lest You Be Judged

Daily Affirmation

I am accepting of others, knowing we are all perfectly made but have acquired wounds to heal

I bet you know what this chapter is about! Judgment! Let's be honest—we've all judged or been judged at some point in our lives. Why *is* that? Why are we *so critical* as a society? To answer this, let's take a moment to recognize what judgment can look and sound like.

In our nation's current political climate of Right vs. Left, I'm certain you can come up with hundreds of judgments; however, let's stick with something a *bit* safer—divorce! A conversation between two friends regarding someone's divorce may go something like this...

> *Did you hear Suzy is leaving Tom? I mean, she has four kids! How could she do that to them? I know, right? I mean, even if Tom does work all the time, he's still a good father and provider. She must be having an affair.* First of all, do we have the facts? Have we spoken on a personal level with Suzy to hear how she feels and what has led her to this decision? Are we afraid to know? Could *Suzy's* reasons potentially be *ours*, unbeknownst to us? Might it be that we could be putting ourselves in Suzy's shoes and imagining "what if…?" as we cast judgment on her?

Consider this: when we're in judgment, are we really just asking ourselves, "Could this be me?"

Let that sink in for a moment.

As we're pondering these questions, here are some other examples that might sound rather familiar. When have we heard or said things like this?

- *Are you sure you don't want to put something else on?*
- *Wow, don't you think your makeup is a bit much?*
- *Did you see those two carrying on like that (being affectionate) in public? They should save it for the bedroom!*

Let's take a moment and focus on the first example, since I happen to have so much experience with it! I can't tell you how many times I've questioned an outfit my daughter was wearing by being passive-aggressive. I thought I was being *tactful*, but her radar for innuendos is as fine-tuned as her momma's, and she knew exactly what I was *really* saying!

I discovered my penchant for being passive-aggressive while on my own healing journey, along with the realization of just how critical I was of others. In fact, I realized that my whole family was critical. In looking back on our family's history, I was able to identify how my ancestors had lived vicariously through others by using gossip to give their stories and lives content and meaning. I wanted to think I had evolved beyond that; however, my eyes were opening to the fact that I, too, wasn't living my own life—and that was being transferred and reflected in the way I parented.

I realized that I was watching others live their lives; in the process, it made mine somehow seem "less," including my family life. I judged others in order to determine for myself if what they were doing was OK, then allowed that to govern whether or not it was acceptable for our family to do the same. In other words, would society be OK with them doing that, wearing that, saying that? If so, then it was acceptable for our family. If not, then judgment was cast, a negative opinion was formed, and passive-aggressive, manipulative comments were made so that things would be done my way, which was obviously society's accepted way.

That mindset resulted in my caring so much about how people might perceive my daughter in *that* outfit that I was willing to risk her self-perception and self-esteem by making the judgmental comments that I made. That wasn't good, nor was it healthy for either of us! Where did that judgment come from?

Let's Make This Personal:
- Take a few minutes to write down some things you judge others about.
- Reflect on what you may be questioning about yourself.

- Ask yourself where in your past you were similarly judged.

Now, let's consider a hypothetical scenario with your spouse. Pretend that you ask your spouse if he forgot to take the trash out. He says "yes," then you judge him for never remembering, which leads into a conversation of "never" and "always."

*You **never** remember!*

*You're **always** taking care of work and not your family!*

*You **never** do anything to help around the house!*

Whoa, hold up…Wait a minute! Is this still about the trash or should you have had a conversation a while ago about something entirely different, and now missing trash day has triggered your anger about this prior issue?

Here's another thought—were you actually judging him for how you feel about some of your own mistakes? Have there been times when you didn't have dinner prepared, clothes washed, or maybe when you didn't make that call you had been putting off? Are you deflecting onto him what you feel about yourself?

We use judgment for any number of things—to feel superior, to mask our shame and guilt, to hurt before being hurt. All of this can lead to feelings of inadequacy, blame, and shame. This is no way to show up in our relationships!

People are human and will understand when we fail to be perfect 100 percent of the time. In fact, they'll appreciate when we're honest, real, vulnerable, and make mistakes, because it makes them feel like they're on equal footing with us.

Begin by letting go of the guilt and shame that causes you to judge others. Accept who you are, failures and flaws, so you can accept others.

If you're surrounded by family, friends, or children who judge, start noticing what they may be judging in themselves. Set the tone of non-judgment by not feeding into their stories and not engaging in their gossip. Show them a different possibility and view of the same circumstance.

For example, let's take another look at that first scenario in which the two friends are gossiping about the divorce of their mutual friend, and consider what it could look like with a different response. This perspective could be offered instead:

> *I believe marriage is one of the most difficult things we can do in life. I'm surprised if any of us get through it unscathed, but the hard times can lead us to greater love. Let's hope things work out well for them and their children.* This simple statement could be enough to stop the gossip and turn the negative energy into a positive outcome of powerful intentions.

Let's Make This Personal:

- Take some time to practice turning judgment into empowerment. When you find yourself in a conversation laden with negativity or gossip, cast a different perspective of compassion and non-judgment as in the statement above.
- As you start turning your judgment around to figure out what you're actually judging in yourself, you'll be met with some healing work. Take the time to journal what you're judging, what's triggering the judgment, and what it's connected to within your heart. It may not be pleasant at first, but will soon lead to a healthier outlook on humanity.

By working through the things that trigger judgment within you, you'll attract more love and compassion into your heart and the hearts of others around you. Stick with it until gossip and judgment become intolerable. When we learn to live *our* truth, we won't succumb to the pressure of living anyone else's. When others try to question your truth, remember: they are judging themselves. It's not about you!

CHAPTER 4

It's Not About YOU!

Daily Affirmation

I am seeing everyone's situation as their own personal journey in finding their truth

One of the biggest struggles for me in my healing journey was understanding that what people thought of me was actually none of my business. I had to realize and accept that when they shared their thoughts with me, it wasn't necessarily about me. I also had to accept that I didn't have to get involved, come up with solutions, or bail them out of what they were going through. Because I have an empathetic personality, I tend to easily take on other people's issues and make them my own. Let me explain by sharing a personal story.

A friend was going through some challenging times with her preteen daughter. At one point, she called me for help, but unfortunately, I was unavailable. I had previously made a decision to set a healthy boundary for myself, and I wanted to honor my friend by not rushing into something that I knew needed more time than I could give at that moment; if I tried to squeeze it in, it would conflict with the boundary I had set. I stated what I could do and when I could do it, and I put the ball back in my friend's court to follow up with me within those parameters.

As soon as I finished speaking with my friend, I immediately felt guilty and thought of all the possible scenarios that could go wrong. I found myself wondering: if they did happen, could I have prevented any of them? I call this state of worry about things that haven't even happened "negative rumination" and liken it to a hamster on a wheel. This kind of thinking can make you feel crazy and can actually cause physical harm to your body!

Fast forward. A month went by, and my friend's situation had actually worsened. Was this my fault because I hadn't been available when she needed me? Could this decline in my friend's daughter have been caused by me? Should I have sacrificed what was important to me to somehow save this child from what she was now going through? Are you thinking, "YES! Yes, you should have prioritized your *friend* over *yourself*, especially to help a child!"

What if I told you that's exactly what I had chosen to do in the past and that I had actually thrived off of rushing in and saving the

You Change, They Change

day in any number of situations, not just ones in my family? I found my identity in portraying my ability to be righteous, good, and the "all-powerful voice of reason" in any situation. I was the *calm in the storm*; the *speaker of truth and justice*. I loved being needed. It gave my life purpose. Wow! I sound like I have the power to cure everything, don't I?

I don't, and I didn't. True healing comes from within. I realized that I could be a vessel to lead people to their truth and help them heal, but when I don't allow them the struggle of doing the work themselves, I rob them of their victory and of their sense of having come out on the other side of the storm stronger, healthier, wiser, and ready to share their hope with others.

I recognized that it was not my place to do the work; it was my friend's. If I kept doing the work for her, I would have created a relationship that was codependent and enabling. By setting a healthy boundary on what I was willing to do and when, I did my part. She chose not to receive my help, and she learned from the experience.

When things get bad enough, people will either rise to the occasion or they won't. In this case, things got worse, but my friend fortunately learned through it. Even now, she's continuing to learn and practice the tools she decided to use during that time in her family's life. I'm immensely proud of her, and of myself for getting out of her way by not thinking she was too weak to do it on her own! I got out of the way, and I didn't make the outcome about me.

Let's look at a situation more commonly experienced by most people. Let's say someone you know posts something on Facebook, and you immediately wonder if it's about you. While certainly sometimes people do post things indirectly about someone in order to state a particular message in not so many words (it's called vaguebooking), more often than not, you were nowhere in their mind when they wrote that particular post.

How do I know this? I've personally experienced it when I've had people call me, angry and upset, about a post they read that had nothing to do with them, a post that no one would have ever associated with them. They were making an incorrect assumption.

Let's think through another example. Let's pretend that your husband came home from work one evening and asked if his pants got picked up from the drycleaners. You immediately assumed it was a dig at your lack of responsibility and started rattling off the list of horrible things that had happened to you that day, trying to excuse why the pants weren't back. Did *he* make it about you or did *you*?

Let's Make This Personal:

- Take a moment and ask yourself: have there been times when you've rescued others to feel more important, better than, or worthy? Write down any examples that come to mind.
- When might you have turned simple questions or comments into a personal attack on your abilities? Write those examples down and try to determine what might have triggered your misperception in those situations. Was it connected to something that had happened in the past?
- Now, ask yourself where you learned that rescuing or getting involved was not only permissible, but encouraged, and journal what comes to mind.
- Finally, practice not being the savior of the day, and remember—it's not about you!
    - Reflect on how it felt to set a healthy boundary and say "no," and what good came from getting out of the way.

So, how do we keep in mind that it's not about us and still be helpful, empathetic, and encouraging? How do we not make things about us and still feel validated? We set healthy boundaries. We outline a clear plan of what needs to happen for us to help. If those things are ignored or not met, then we realize they didn't actually want our help. They wanted us to fix their problem, which may be a repetition of similar issues that have happened in some form or another throughout the course of their entire lives.

In my case, I finally realized that my friend would keep repeating the same problematic behavior if I didn't allow her the opportunity to have her "ah-ha moment" of clarity in which she learned to be proactive instead of reactive. Once she got in a better place to receive enlightenment, real positive change could occur.

In short, if I had not set the boundary I did when I did, my friend's daughter may not be here now. My friend may not have had the awakening she had, and I wouldn't be able to tell you that you need to get out of the way for people to be able to do the work that they need to do themselves.

Remember—it's not about you! It's not yours to fix! Instead of jumping through hoops to "help," I learned to send life preservers to keep my friend and her daughter afloat and headed in the right direction to shore. I encouraged other family members to do the same. I had to learn to "let go and let God."

Now, let's talk about feeling worthy, validated, and needed. By now, I hope you're realizing that the only person you need to validate you is YOU! Let's just pretend that Facebook comment *was* aimed at you. If you're operating with intention and owning your truth, then you don't have to give that post one ounce of your energy. If you feel you need to clean up a mess you may have made, ask yourself why. Write down the possible scenarios related to facing this person, along with the potential outcomes. Talk it out with your spouse or with a friend you trust in order to determine what good, if any, could come from confronting a Facebook message that may or may not have been about you, then take your next steps from there.

Honestly, I think you already know your next steps. If someone isn't sure enough of their truth to confront you with it, then it's probably not a good idea for you to engage or discuss it with them. Let go and let God! What you feed energy into grows. Make sure you send compassion and love instead of worry and stress.

As for the example of your hubby's pants still being at the drycleaners, you could instead respond with, "No, I didn't get to it today. They do open early in the morning. If it's something you need for tomorrow, you can pick them up. If not, I'll set myself a reminder to do it then."

Notice there was no explanation of why the pants didn't get picked up. You don't need to have an excuse to validate that his pants weren't on your priority list today. Now that you know it's important to him, you can choose to make it important to you. Wouldn't you want the same from him?

This is straight talk—not guilting or shaming each other! It's owning your truth without explanation or a need for validation from anyone other than yourself. If you were asked to get the pants and you agreed and didn't do it, then apologize and ask yourself why. Did you agree to something you didn't want to do? Did you know when you said you would get the pants that it would be a problem or burden for you? Was it an issue of having overextended yourself, and leaving his pants there was the least costly thing on your list to not get done?

This is where healthy boundaries can benefit us greatly. We're such a quick response society, with technology capable of connecting us in seconds, that we tend to feel rushed into decisions. We don't have to be! If you aren't sure you can do something, you can simply say, "I'll get back to you on that" or "I'm not available to answer that at this time." Think of the freedom our teens would experience if they felt they didn't have to respond to their messages the instant the notification dinged! It's the same feeling, just different circumstances.

"It's not about you" is the most freeing thought process! Start practicing by saying it as often as you need to, and follow that by rewriting the story in your head that supports it as opposed to the one that feeds stress and worry. If this is a difficult task, it may be time to look in the mirror.

CHAPTER 5

Look in The Mirror

Daily Affirmation

I am understanding of myself and others, with love and acceptance

Now that we've established that it's not about us unless we are directly involved in a situation, we have more time. We have a newfound freedom to honor ourselves and find our passions. Unfortunately, this is when we sometimes start to subconsciously sabotage ourselves for lack of self-esteem. We're so disconnected from our wants and needs that we end up finding ourselves focusing on what others are not changing in themselves.

Take some time and journal your answers to these two questions:

1. What negativity do you keep focusing on?
2. What change in your life are you waiting for before you will feel free to move forward?

Sometimes we can become so focused on what everyone else is doing wrong that we stop ourselves from doing what's right. We complain about the same things over and over and blame the same individuals or circumstances without effecting positive change.

This can happen a great deal in marriage. Let's take a look at my personal favorite example. Let's say that a couple agrees they need help with their marriage. They go through a few counseling sessions of blaming, shaming, and making excuses for their behaviors, which results in them not getting anywhere positive. They're so busy focusing on the faults in the other person that they're unable to see that they're complaining about the exact same things in each other! They are, in fact, the complete mirror image of one another. How can we snap them out of that? We give them the tools to change!

In this case, it's a literal handheld mirror, and yes, I've had one! My husband was even instructed to buy it for me! My instructions were to look into it whenever I spoke to anyone at home. Did I like my mirror? NO! I had a deep hatred for it. I didn't like seeing myself, my weaknesses, and the ways in which I was responsible for my problems.

Fortunately, my mirror made me stronger in the end. The fact of the matter was that I hadn't been owning my truth, and the mirror exercise helped me to recognize that. I discovered I was people-pleasing instead of "Kim pleasing." I was putting everyone else's needs before mine and then resenting *them* for it! Sound familiar? Let me give you some other personal examples that may help you to identify this behavior in yourself.

One of my pet peeves is using cell phones to communicate while sitting in the same room, at the same table. In the past, my husband and daughter would both be at the table with their cell phones out, using them to drive a conversation with each other, every sentence having a reference to something they saw on the internet. It was their way of connecting, but far from mine. I would feel left out and even angry and disconnected when they would spend a dinner communicating this way. However, when I would get a text from a client, I was instantly engaged on my phone. It was the same disconnect, albeit for different reasons, but still a mirror image.

In another scenario, I wanted my husband to be more passionate about my business. I asked him to let me come talk to his work staff about wellness so that I could introduce them to the tools that have helped our family. I wanted him to buy into what I was passionate about and to tell others.

When he didn't respond as I had expected him to, I thought about where the disconnect was, and I realized that I hadn't actually sold him on using the tools. This is why he wasn't passionate about promoting them with his staff. We weren't using them in every area we could in our daily routine. We weren't being products of the product. Plus, my lack of educating him on their benefits and uses made him wary of educating others, because he wasn't personally equipped to do so.

Once I recognized my failure to empower him with the tools he needed, I became less defensive and started being more proactive, opening up his mind to the uses of plant-based medicine in his work life and daily routines. He noticed the positive changes and so did his employees. As a result, they started asking him about the tools he used. He became a product of the product when I gave him the opportunity to do so without my judgment or attachment to the outcome.

Take some time to journal your responses to the following prompts:

- Are you accusing others of the same things you're doing? If you discover that you are, write down some examples.
- Where in the past have you seen that behavior in others?
- Consider buying a mirror and making some personal discoveries. Journal the feelings and thoughts that break free when you watch yourself throughout your daily life, reflected in a mirror.
  - Try to see what others see when they look at you, and journal your reflections.
  - See what you see in them reflected back on you. What does that look like to you?

Another lesson that came from my mirror was insight on how I interacted with my daughter. I realized I was walking on eggshells to make her happy, and I did that at my own expense as well as hers. Where else in life were people going to do this for her? Nowhere! I needed to stop my behavior so that she wasn't set up for failure in life, thinking that everyone else would jump through hoops to meet her demands. Let me give you an example of what I'm talking about.

My daughter texted me from school asking, "Mom, after school can I go get my nails done for the dance with my friends and you pick me up when I'm done?" I said, "Yes, but give me a heads up before you're ready for me to get you. It's about a fifteen-minute drive at that time of day."

She finished and texted that she was ready for me to pick her up. I headed out about ten minutes later. She called me as soon as I was heading down our driveway, asking with some anxiety, "Where are you?! My friends are waiting to leave because they don't want to leave me here alone." Now, I'm feeling anxious and guilty for not being there.

Wait! *WHAT?! NO!* I didn't know to go get her until she called. I'm not telepathic. My end was clean. I also didn't ask for the others to stay and wait for her to be picked up. That was very nice of them and I'm sure five minutes more wasn't going to put them out; however, in my daughter's mind it was a big deal and this current situation was all my fault. In turn, I accepted my punishment by arguing back and forth with her over who was to blame for the miscommunication. This was not healthy, not good!

So, what is my mirror reflection in this scenario? When have I acted as my daughter acted? Why did I get so irritated with her behavior? Was I free from blame?

I looked back on this scenario after the fact and realized I hadn't thought through my response to her original question. I hadn't asked for details because I was working on something I wanted to finish, and her getting her nails done would give me that extra time. I was rushed and feeling overwhelmed, and I snapped when my daughter snapped.

My daughter had also taken advantage of my distraction and not provided me with necessary details regarding her nail excursion. She got anxious and overwhelmed and she snapped. We were both to blame—me, for leaving later than I should have; my daughter, for not giving me a timely heads up. This example may sound silly, but even these insignificant life events can turn into small wounds that add up.

My daughter and I can set each other off with just a look. Why is that? It's because we see the worst in ourselves reflected back to each other. It's not pretty sometimes, but it's necessary to recognize and grow from each experience. Leading by example is the biggest lesson I can give her. Setting healthy boundaries by saying no, letting her know that I'll get back to her when I've had a minute to think, or telling her that I need more information would be a great start. Teaching my teenager and myself to think things through before either of us commits to something is an important life lesson to master. When you're pressured and don't set these types of healthy boundaries, that's when you may find yourself shaming someone, and when you need to think about why you are deflecting blame.

Our teens are subject to as much, if not more, stress than we are each day. Their need to please at a moment's notice is heightened by the electronic age of instant communication, creating greater anxiety. Where are they seeing this in us? Do we just as automatically disengage from our time with them so we may be there for everyone else? I know this was a big revelation for me. The very thing I was accusing my husband of doing to me—using his phone and prioritizing his work—I was doing to my daughter and her to me.

Let your family know you're using a mirror in conversations with them in order to better see and understand what they see when you speak to them. Tell them how you want them to see you. Explain that you're using the mirror to become more aware of what you're reflecting because you want to be the best example and leader for them to mirror.

Use your mirror to dig deep and see yourself with all your vulnerabilities. Use your mirror to strengthen your weaknesses and heal your wounds. A simple mirror can change your perception, change how you're perceived by others, and set the tone for how you want to show up in the world. It's time we set positive examples and speak a new language of love and compassion that communicates that we're all the same.

CHAPTER 6

Speaking a New Language

Daily Affirmation

I know who I am and what I want and am keeping my focus on what's good and positive

Self-love and self-care leads to inner truth, which becomes outward vulnerability, leading to open hearts that tear down walls.

Let's break this down.

First, self-love—what is it and what does it look like? For us to have self-love, we have to know ourselves and be able to tap into our passions, convictions, wants, hopes, and dreams. Journal the following:

- *What do you want?*
- *Who are you?*
- *What do you want to be?*

I know a lot of us lose who we are as a result of trying to fit into the mold we feel society or our parents and generations before have placed us in. *Did they really? Or did we perceive that they did?* Was it our fear of not being what or whom we thought others wanted us to be that stopped us from being who we were meant to be?

Let that sink in.

- Did you perceive that you needed to be a certain way to please your nearest and dearest?
- Was that perception the basis of who you became?

Take the time to write some notes in your journal on these questions and the lies you may have told yourself that now make you feel stuck.

Some examples of these perceived lies could include thoughts such as these: "I'm not pretty enough to get a date. I'm not smart enough to get into that school. I'm not patient enough to have children. I have a learning disability, a spending problem, addictive behavior so I can't …" You get the picture.

Did we assume a role they gave us because it was a good excuse not to change? Not to be better than? Not to try to be something more, something truer to whom we knew we were created to be? Do you think it could have been their way of controlling us? Scaring us into submission? Or was it our convenient perception of the truth that kept us from trying, because in trying, we risked failure?

All of this starts at a very young age. You may still notice yourself doing it at times. Does any of this sound familiar?

"Don't cut your hair short. You look better with long hair."

"You can't date him; he looks different and hangs out with the wrong crowd."

"You honestly think you can make a career out of *singing*?"

I could rattle off more examples, but I'd rather you write down some of your own in your journal, along with your answers to the questions above.

Now, let's take a moment to reflect on why we're still speaking those words to ourselves, subconsciously allowing them to control us and keep us stuck, paralyzed in fear of failure or fear of success. Let's take the above examples and turn each of them around.

"I'm going to try short hair. Maybe it will look fabulous. If not, it will grow back."

"Maybe he does look different from me, but I feel God leading me to be his friend. Maybe he will turn out to be very interesting and a good person." In contrast, even if the person turned out to be a bad fit for you, at least you would know instead of spending valuable time wondering.

"Maybe I will be able to make enough money singing to build a center for talented youth. Or maybe I won't make much money singing, but my trying will lead me to a fascinating job I've never imagined."

See how perception can change anything into a positive? Self-love means finding your truth and living by it with conviction and passion despite what you perceive others' opinions to be.

So, how does inner truth become outward vulnerability, opening your heart and breaking down walls? To explain, I'll give you a personal example.

My forty-sixth birthday was on a Wednesday. The weekend before had come and gone with no mention of any celebratory activities. I had voiced that we should do something, but no plans were made due to bad weather. No worries; we still had another weekend, since my actual birthday was in the middle of the week.

I had the forethought to schedule my day with time in the middle for self-care. I scheduled a one-hour Reiki session and lunch with my teenage daughter. The day had gone well and I was happy with my cards and present from my hubby. It was nothing extravagant, but it was very thoughtful. He actually had to be sneaky and go out of his way to get it done, so I was impressed!

Back to that lunch…I hadn't realized when I planned my day that my daughter would be in the middle of an exam week and stressed out hormonally. She was no fun to be around! More than that, she just wasn't nice. It was *my birthday* and she was being self-absorbed and ruining my happiness!

Then, I rushed home for my last client of the day, who ended up being twenty minutes late, and who needed lots of my energy. By the time I was done, I had forgotten all the good things that had happened that day and labeled the whole birthday as a bad one. I was in a funk of negativity. I even started thinking badly of my husband for not planning anything, even though he had bought me a thoughtful gift, asked if I wanted to go out to dinner or if I preferred he bring something home, and even bought me a gluten-free cake and a candle to blow out!

What was my problem? I was forty-six, not eight!

Did I expect everyone and everything to know it was my day, so they should stop living theirs? Could I have controlled everyone to do *exactly* what I wanted them to do to make me feel loved and cared for on *my birthday*?! No, I could not. I could only control *me*—my perception, my attitude, my outcome.

I could have used my daughter's attitude as an opportunity to ask her open-ended questions that would lead her to the root of why she was feeling upset. Or, I could have spoken to her about naming things she was grateful for to help raise her spirits and her frequency to a positive vibration. That surely would have raised mine!

I could have set a clear boundary with my client, letting her know that we had to end on time despite the fact that she had been caught in traffic. I could have arranged to speak to her over the phone, following up another day. I would have had more time to gather my thoughts and feelings, figure out what I wanted the rest of my evening to look like, and ask for it.

Instead, I was so aggravated that I isolated myself. My poor husband tried to do what I wanted, but I really didn't know what that was. I didn't want anything from anyone except for them to listen to me complain!

Sound familiar? Where have you seen this in yourself?

Upon reflection on my day, I became vulnerable to change. I told my husband I wasn't disappointed in him or my gifts or even in not going anywhere. Instead, I was disappointed in myself for not personally using the tools I equip others with—empowering them, but not myself. Employing vulnerability and self-reflection, instead of blaming and shaming my husband, my daughter, or my client, spoke volumes to me. It also allowed my husband to not feel like a failure, or like he needed to fix something. I actually let him off the hook by telling him he couldn't win!

> *You can't win here. It's not anything you're doing or not doing. I'm miserable and I'm aware it's on me. Just love me and validate me and let me vent.*

He did. He didn't shame me or get defensive. He gave me the space I needed and a loving hug, tearing down the wall. In the end, I knew it was up to me to turn my birthday story around. I clearly said what I wanted the following weekend to look like and what I wanted to do. When things didn't go exactly as I had pictured, I rerouted my brain to see the positive in what was happening instead.

I loved the growth and the reminder that came from this day, May 24, 2017. It was the day I remembered why, in the past, my husband or my children may not have felt like they were good enough. I needed to remember this for myself and so I could teach you. Don't let your lack of knowing who you are and what you want, or a lack of self-care, be the cause of an unhealthy relationship with the people you love the most. A bad day can just be a bad day. It doesn't have to be anyone's fault. You can decide to focus on the positive and be grateful instead of hateful.

So, what then is self-care? Self-care is taking care of your physical, mental, and spiritual growth so that you can find your personal truth. When we're not centered, grounded, and focused on our truth, we can lose sight of who we are and what we want. When we practice self-care, we're able to tap into our higher power and be enlightened to our soul's purpose.

Let's Make This Personal:

- What are some things you do for self-care?
- What are some things you could do more consistently?
- In addition to this chapter's meditation, you will find links on my website, www.kimmcdonnel.com, to videos of my Mindful Movements class and tapping and breathing exercises. These are some of the tools I use for my self-care.

Now that you've seen the real you, you are better equipped to stop the blaming, shaming, and defensive behavior. You're now ready to evoke real change. As we've learned, these reactions come from lack of self-truth, self-esteem, and courage. How do we attain those things when the voice in our heads has been beating us up? The simple answer is gratitude and a positive mindset—focusing on the good instead of the bad, the positive instead of the negative. Does this mean bad things won't happen? No, but now you'll have these tools to evoke positive energy and turn your perception around.

I know, you're asking yourself, "How? Kim, have *you* ever been able to do that yourself in a really horrible situation?" The answer to that is yes, and this is how:

Faith!

Through faith in a higher power, you'll believe all things are possible and actually orchestrated to work out, even in death—that there's a bigger purpose and reason for everything. But you need to choose to believe that for yourself when you're ready. When you open your mind to this possibility, you release yourself from worry, stress and the need to control. What have you got to lose? What you will gain is time, energy, and a positive outlook on life.

Assuming the worst and ruminating on negative thoughts will only rob you of the joy of living. Dr. Edward Bach wrote one of my favorite quotes, which I once found most frustrating:

> *Once we come to the realization that we are beyond pain and suffering, beyond care or worry or fear, beyond everything except the joy of life, the joy of death, and the joy of our immortality, we can walk that path through any danger, through any difficulty, unafraid.*

Having faith over fear and practicing gratitude gives you the ability to rewrite the story in your head.

CHAPTER 7

Rewrite Your Story

Daily Affirmation

I am seeing my past as the perfect canvas to paint the picture of who I am now, full of compassion, joy, and love

At this point, you realize that our truth is what we perceive it to be. If the truth you're telling yourself makes you upset, frustrated, sick, and stuck, learning to rewrite it can turn your life around!

Have you ever met someone who only talks about the bad things? Such a "woe is me" mentality is hard to be around. Every good idea you give that person to help themselves is met with another excuse to stay sick, stuck, or frustrated. Isn't that annoying?

Take a moment to journal responses to the following questions:

- When have you noticed these "woe is me" qualities in someone, and how do you feel around that person? Do you avoid them or feel exhausted after speaking to them? In what ways does their outlook affect your emotions?
- What about you? Are you guilty of being a martyr, victim, or negative person? Think about your past behaviors and responses. When have you spoken negatively in your life? What has been the catalyst for any negative responses you may have had?

Start noticing when you speak negatively. If watching the news or being in contact with negativity makes you excited, like you're a part of a group, it must be giving you something you want—community, perhaps? A feeling of belonging to something, a cause or a movement? Or could it be the need to figure things out?

In searching for our answers, we can sometimes question everything. This can be perceived as being negative if the delivery of our questions is not well received. Let me share my personal experience about being what my mom called a whiner.

When I was a little girl, my older sister was very jealous of me. She made my life miserable with hateful words and mean looks. She couldn't stand to be around me—but if I went away from her, she couldn't stand that either. I was in a constant state of push and pull. One minute she liked me because she wanted me to play, and the next minute she didn't. I felt good when she wanted me and not good when she didn't.

This was a codependent relationship full of discord. I didn't know how to stop the cycle. I'd beg my mom for help, but in words that sounded like whining to her. She didn't receive my message because I couldn't articulate my feelings to her. All I could say was "She is being mean to me" in a whining voice.

My mom was told by books on parenting to "let the kids work it out, it will teach them life lessons." I took that as abandonment. I was being tortured and asking for support, and no one was listening. I wasn't validated for my feelings; I was shamed for them.

This pattern stuck with me in life until my very recent adulthood. I had to look in that mirror and find my voice—not the negative, whiny voice that wasn't getting heard. I had to find my truth. I needed to know who I was and what I was made to be before I could articulate what I wanted and needed.

The truth is, I liked playing with my sister and wanted the good to never turn into the bad. I wanted to control my sister's being mean to me by making it my mom's problem instead of fixing how I responded and engaged with her. Although I can't go back to fix those years, my sister and I both can do better to help our girls know how to have a voice in their relationships. I'm happy to say that my sister and I love and respect each other very much, and our children are reaping the benefits of our hard-fought lessons.

I realize now why I wasn't being heard, and why this pattern stuck with me in jobs and relationships. I always attracted or called into my life people who were "heard," people who would question what I was asking for or what I was saying. I would feel bullied. I didn't have a comeback. I eventually didn't have a voice in any situation because it was easier to give up and give in to their wishes, even in trivial situations, like being asked for where I wanted to eat only to be persuaded to choose differently.

I was not whom I wanted to be because I didn't think I was smart enough to have a say. The personalities I chose to align with were bigger than mine, smarter than mine, and could feel good about themselves by taking care of me, the victim.

As horrible as I can feel about that time in my life, I am grateful for the lessons it brought me—the resiliency and strength, the voice that can be clear, honored, and heard. I don't blame the people who came into my life to teach me these lessons. I honor them for the role they played in getting me here. I now know how to handle a bully with compassion and empathy, and without losing my voice. See how I just turned that negative past into a positive story of change?

This one is tough! If you're "a glass half empty" person, it will be difficult to rewrite a more positive story than the one playing in your head. It's going to take filling your mind with positivity and gratitude to get out of your negative self-talk.

Let's make this personal by using these suggested activities:

- Practice positivity by journaling three things you are grateful for each day.
- Use this chapter's online meditation any time you feel you are unable to see the positive.
- Practice changing your negative perception when ruminating on negative thoughts. Focus on the good in order to outweigh the bad.
- Start practicing rewriting other people's scenarios when they come to you with a negative outlook.

Let's take a look at an example:

Let's say your husband's plane is delayed two hours, and he'll most likely miss his connecting flight. There's nothing more he can do to change the circumstances, and he's forced to wait and see what will happen. He can choose to be aggravated—constantly complaining to everyone around him about how it's going to negatively impact his day, and calling you to complain in kind.

Instead of pouring more negativity into a situation he can't change, you can choose to help him rewrite his story. Ask him open-ended questions about what he can do to make this time purposeful and if there are some things he's put off due to lack of time. Tell him to take the time to relax, breathe, meditate with headphones on, and focus on letting go of any negativity. Suggest a chair massage or a shoeshine to relax and distract him from the delay. Tell him he is meant to be there at this time, in that place, for a purpose. Paint a picture of how his time can be spent and what positive impact that can have on him and the people around him who are also frustrated about the delay. Once he reframes his perception, others can choose to follow, creating a more positive environment for all.

How would this way of responding be a change from the ways in which you would normally respond, especially in this circumstance? Think about it for a moment. Would you normally say something about how his delay is going to negatively affect you and the plans you had for him? Would you have stated a list of things that now need to be rearranged that will add to his negativity and frustration?

Sometimes when we process new information out loud, we dump our anger and frustration onto someone else who is already angry and frustrated. When you turn off your mindset of negativity, you create a channel for positivity to not only impact you, but all those with whom you come in contact. You can choose to accept that things happen and that you've got to let things go and roll with the punches. You can choose to accept them as an opportunity for growth or just an interesting experience, or you can accept them as an opportunity to be angry and wallow in self-pity.

So, why is it so hard to choose positivity over negativity? It's because we're actually hard-wired to be negative. Being on guard, worried, and stressed is the norm in our busy society with its emphasis on getting ahead. We don't take the time to be grateful for where we are and mindful of where we want to be; to enjoy our life and all its benefits. Being hard-wired for negativity served our ancestors well to survive; however, we've evolved past the need to be in fight-or-flight mode, always waiting for the next drama.

As I stated before, what you put energy into grows. Grow your positivity, negate the fear and anxiety keeping you from happiness, and rewrite your story to be what you want it to be! You choose your reality. You can rewrite your story to be one of purpose, meaning, and abundance if you believe you can. Just try! What have you got to lose?

Want to know what you'll gain when you do rewrite your story? You'll walk in love and compassion, radiating positivity and receiving positivity. You'll attract good people and opportunities, and you'll be successful in all areas of life. It really is that simple!

When fear loses, success can win.

CHAPTER 8

Defining Success

Daily Affirmation

I am successfully living a balanced life full of love and acceptance

By now, you may be wondering if "they" will change once you have taken steps toward changing yourself. That's a fair question, although true success comes from letting go of the need to know.

As you learned in the previous chapters, when you have INTEGRITY and live your TRUTH, seeking FAITH over FEAR and practicing GRATITUDE, you'll be truly, successfully living a balanced life. If the people in your life aren't doing the same or are uncomfortable with your positive changes, know that it's not your journey or your timing that's the problem, but theirs. Pray that their hearts will be open to change, and make the tools that you've used available to them.

This book and other books I've listed on my website are great tools to give to people on this journey. Guided meditations to assist in opening the mind to the divine are also on my website to share. These tools will let them know they are loved and cared for, but that you're not compromising who you are to make them comfortable any longer.

The example I use to help people understand this concept further is my family's eating. When I was diagnosed with MS at age forty, I began changing to an autoimmune diet. I was not changing anyone else's diet; however, some of my immediate family had issues with how I ate.

I come from an Italian family that shows love and affection by feeding you enormous amounts of unhealthy, carb and sugar-laden food. They took my food sensitivity as a personal affront instead of seeing it as my need to survive and thrive. The more I fed into their issues and argued my point, the further divided we became.

I realized that in trying to convince them, I was really not convinced myself. I was desperate not to have my old habits of eating return, but letting go of food addictions was hard. Once I accomplished my goal of feeling healthier through better food choices and plant-based supplements, I knew my truth, and it was much easier to live it peacefully. I didn't have to convince myself or anyone else. I could lead by example. My taste buds no longer enjoyed the processed foods I once craved.

Did that change them? Some of them, yes. The others have their own journey to take on their road to letting go of codependent food behavior. Living with debilitating pain and the possibility of paralysis and loss of life were the hammers hitting me over the head.

I can't expect anyone to change their life based on my journey; however, in my house, I don't supply the harmful foods to my family, and they're happy I don't. This was not an overnight transition. My son was graduating high school at the time of my diagnosis with MS. Going to college can present obstacles to maintaining a healthy diet. My son was met with his own challenges and learned for himself how lifestyle changes could positively impact how he felt physically and mentally. This has now extended to my son's family and is having a positive impact on my grandchildren. They are being exposed to healthier lifestyles than my generation was even aware of. This creates positive changes for generations to come. I'm so proud of my son for being the positive change in his family. I'm so grateful I had the tools to give him based on my own journey to health.

I did this through explaining, not shaming; asking questions, not assuming I knew the answers; and allowing others to know their truth while staying faithful to mine. Live and let live, love and let go, let go and let God. It's not my job to save the world from itself. It's my conviction to tell those open to listening about what has worked for me.

My success is not your success. The true definition of success is when you can lay your head down peacefully every night knowing that you are living life to the fullest with intention and faith. It's also owning your truth and setting healthy boundaries with those who don't respect or own theirs.

Leading by example and being open to receive divine guidance daily will allow you to walk through life without fear or judgment, spreading compassion and love to all you meet. Your positive thoughts and acts of gratitude will repel the negative and attract those who are on the journey with you. Be faithful in your practice, especially when it's hard. Those are the times you grow the most!

ABOUT THE AUTHOR

Kim is a Holistic Health Coach and Spiritual Counselor. Through her own journey to healing Kim found success in letting go. After 10 years of medical diagnoses with no cure, debilitating pain, and bouts of depression Kim was introduced to holistic health. In working with a Naturopathic Doctor Kim saw results which gave her hope. Her healing journey took her back to the root cause of all dis-ease to focus on the spiritual journey of the mind body connection.

At age 41 Kim started facilitating the biofeedback scans that brought her so much healing. She noticed that a recurring theme impacting health was our need to control. The stress of controlling every outcome was the true cause of dis-ease. Her journey continued as she was also encouraging others to struggle through the once painful art of healing. With each setback there became a step forward in growth and awareness.

Kim has impacted many lives with her encouraging words and ability to meet people where they are and grow them into the person they want to be. Her desire to heal is inspiring others to do the same. In writing this book she hopes to reach many more who want to make the journey to true healing and evoke positive change on a global scale.

Find her website at www.kimmcdonnel.com

In Gratitude to You

Thank you for your generosity in purchasing You Change, They Change.

I would be so grateful if you could take a minute or two to share what you loved about this book and provide an honest review on our Amazon sales page.

www.ingramcontent.com/pod-product-compliance
Lightning Source LLC
Chambersburg PA
CBHW050508120526
44588CB00044B/1765